GROWING UP GORILLA

HOW A ZOO BABY BROUGHT HER FAMILY TOGETHER

CLARE HODGSON MEEKER

M MILLBROOK PRESS • MINNEAPOLIS

TO JUDY, HARMONY, AND ALL THE GORILLA CARETAKERS WHOSE DEDICATION
AND DEEP RESPECT FOR THESE AMAZING ANIMALS IS INSPIRING

Millbrook Press™
An imprint of Lerner Publishing Group, Inc.
241 First Avenue North
Minneapolis, MN 55401 USA

For reading levels and more information, look up this title at www.lernerbooks.com.

Main body text set in Metro Office.
Typeface provided by Linotype AG.

Library of Congress Cataloging-in-Publication Data

Names: Meeker, Clare Hodgson, author.
Title: Growing up gorilla : how a zoo baby brought her family together / Clare Hodgson Meeker.
Description: Minneapolis : Millbrook Press, [2020] | Audience: Age 10–14. | Audience: Grade 4 to 6.
    | Includes bibliographical references and index.
Identifiers: LCCN 2018052604 (print) | LCCN 2018053089 (ebook) | ISBN 9781541562592 (eb pdf) |
    ISBN 9781541542402 (lb : alk. paper)
Subjects: LCSH: Gorilla—Anecdotes—Juvenile literature. | Mother and child—Juvenile literature. |
    Family reunification—Juvenile literature.
Classification: LCC QL795.G7 (ebook) | LCC QL795.G7 M44 2020 (print) | DDC 599.884—dc23

LC record available at https://lccn.loc.gov/2018052604

Manufactured in the United States of America
1-45407-39520-1/22/2019

CONTENTS

CHAPTER 1
FIRSTBORN

A steady November rain drummed on the roof of the gorilla dens at Seattle's Woodland Park Zoo. Inside, a nineteen-year-old gorilla named Nadiri was preparing to give birth. She'd spent a restless night gathering a thick nest of hay around her, but she could not lie still for more than a few minutes. Even the burlap sack she used as a blanket could not soothe her to sleep.

Harmony Frazier, the infant-care expert at the zoo, had spent a sleepless night too. She was excited to see the gorilla she had helped raise have her first baby. Nineteen years earlier, Nadiri's mother had rejected her after a difficult birth. Harmony had taken care of Nadiri for nine months until an adult female in another gorilla family at the zoo became a surrogate, or substitute, mother to her. Now it was Nadiri's turn to be a mother. Would she take care of her baby?

Harmony could tell the labor pains were getting stronger as she watched Nadiri toss hay in the air and move around in her den. A few times, the weary mother-to-be came over and leaned her head against the metal fencing that separated the two of them. "It's going to be okay, Nadi," Harmony whispered as she reached her fingers through the holes in the webbing to comfort her old friend.

SURROGATE PARENTS

All primate babies need someone to care for them. Primates include monkeys, apes, and humans. Most of the time, a mother ape or monkey cares for her baby. But when she can't, the baby needs a surrogate mother.

"The most natural thing for a baby gorilla is to be held," says Barbara Jones, one of the lead coordinators of a pioneering surrogacy program at the Columbus Zoo in Ohio. She and Maureen Casale have spent the past twenty years caring for gorilla infants whose mothers have died or cannot care for them. They've helped introduce the infants to surrogate gorilla families. What is the secret to their success?

"We follow what the gorillas do," says Maureen.

"Gorillas are very family oriented," adds Barb. "We watch what those who are good mothers do and emulate them."

"But the happiest time for us," says Maureen, "is when they're with a surrogate gorilla mom and it's successful." Even in the wild, surrogate parenting can happen when another adult female gorilla in a family group takes over the care of an orphaned infant.

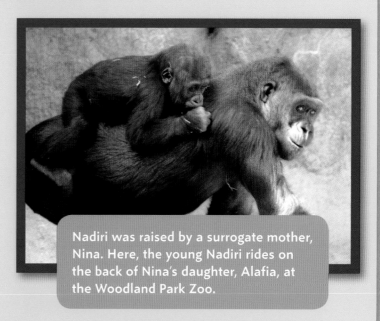

Nadiri was raised by a surrogate mother, Nina. Here, the young Nadiri rides on the back of Nina's daughter, Alafia, at the Woodland Park Zoo.

Nadiri's baby would be the first gorilla born at the zoo in eight years. With fewer than one hundred thousand western lowland gorillas left in the world, every gorilla birth is important.

Gorilla keeper Judy Sievert came over to check on Nadiri's progress during her morning routine of feeding the other gorillas. Like Harmony, Judy had helped care for Nadiri since she had been a baby. In the few months before the birth, Judy had worked with her to practice picking up and holding a burlap doll. "Would Nadiri use this mothering behavior," she wondered, "when the right moment came?"

Together, Judy and Harmony followed the waves of Nadiri's contractions throughout the morning. Finally, just before noon, Nadiri lay down and gave birth in the deep nest she'd made. Harmony listened for the soft squawking sound of a newborn gorilla, but she heard nothing. No one could see the baby through the high wall of hay.

Infant animal care specialist Harmony Frazier holds a picture of Nadiri's baby. Harmony had helped hand-raise Nadiri and her sister Akenji at Woodland Park Zoo.

Keeper Judy Sievert started as a volunteer at Woodland Park Zoo in 1978. In six years, she worked her way up and has been a gorilla keeper ever since.

A very pregnant Nadiri takes a short rest in the nest she made a day before the birth.

"It's hard to see if the baby is moving or not," Harmony said to Darin Collins, the zoo's head veterinarian, who was standing by at the birth. They all held their breath, waiting for the new mother to pick up her baby and clean her off, as a gorilla mother in the wild would.

But a few moments later, Nadiri stood up and looked confused, as if she did not understand what had just happened. Then she walked to the other side of the den with empty arms.

This was not what the staff hoped would happen, but they had prepared for the possibility Nadiri wouldn't immediately bond with her baby. They had no time to lose—they needed to check on the baby.

"What if fluids are blocking the baby's airway?" asked Harmony. "We need to make sure that the newborn is okay."

The keepers closed a sliding door to separate Nadiri from the baby so that Darin could give her a quick checkup. He dried off the infant and gently suctioned a little fluid from her airway. "It's a girl! Her vital signs look good and she is completely healthy," he announced with a smile of relief.

The newborn gorilla weighed 5 pounds (2.3 kg). She had long, spindly arms, ten fingers and ten toes, big brown eyes, and a heart-shaped nose. Darin wrapped her in a warm fleece blanket and handed her to Harmony.

Holding the tiny infant in her arms reminded Harmony of Nadiri as a baby. Nadiri had spent most of her first year of life being hand-raised by humans in a nursery away from other gorillas. But now zookeepers know that young gorillas learn best by watching and imitating the older gorillas around them.

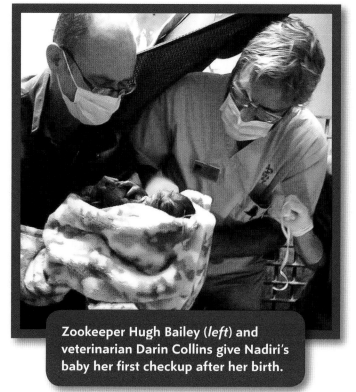

Zookeeper Hugh Bailey (*left*) and veterinarian Darin Collins give Nadiri's baby her first checkup after her birth.

"The best way for this baby to learn to act like a gorilla would be to have her own mother care for her surrounded by her gorilla family," Harmony thought. The baby needed to know from the start that she was a gorilla, not a human.

Harmony and the gorilla-care team were determined to help Nadiri bond with her baby. If they could get her to feel comfortable enough with the baby to pick her up and nurse her, maybe her maternal, or mothering, instinct would kick in. But if not, they would eventually have to find a female gorilla at another zoo to adopt her. There was no other female at the Woodland Park Zoo who was the right age and temperament to care for her.

MOTHERING IS A LEARNED BEHAVIOR

In the past, zoos around the country hand-raised gorilla infants in sterile nurseries, away from other gorillas. Experts had thought it was the safest and healthiest way to keep the infant alive when a gorilla mother rejected her baby. Sadly, many mother gorillas in zoos rejected their babies because they had never seen how a gorilla mother cares for her young. According to Woodland Park Zoo mammal curator Martin Ramirez, gorillas, like humans, learn parenting and other life skills from being parented or from watching others do it. Today, thanks to what gorillas have shown us, zoos are changing gorilla-infant care from a human-centered environment to a gorilla-centered one.

Western lowland gorilla Imbi holds her newborn gorilla at the zoo in Belo Horizonte, Brazil, in May 2017.

Nadiri's newborn gorilla clutches the burlap sack she is wrapped in with her tiny fingers.

The tiny infant clung to Harmony's fleece vest, which looked and felt like gorilla fur. "She has a strong grip," Harmony thought. That was a good sign. The safest place for a baby gorilla in the wild is clinging to her mother's chest. At two hours old, this infant already seemed to know she'd have to hold on tight to survive.

CHAPTER 2
HOME IN THE GORILLA DENS

Nadiri's baby has a distinctive heart-shaped nose. Western lowland gorillas have differently shaped noseprints and lips than other gorilla subspecies.

The first few days are critical in a newborn gorilla's life. In the wild, mother gorillas carry their babies with them all the time to make sure that they are warm, safe, and well fed. But when the keepers tried placing the baby back in Nadiri's den, the new mother kept her distance and made no move to pick her up.

"If we have any hope of Nadiri becoming a mother, this baby needs to be part of her everyday life," said Judy. The keepers decided to let Nadiri rest while they prepared a separate den where Harmony would care for the baby. It was right next to Nadiri's den, so she could see her baby day and night. It was also within sight of the other gorillas.

"Welcome home," Harmony whispered to the tiny infant as she carried her into her new den. Harmony had helped raise more than one hundred baby animals, from black bear and snow leopard cubs to wolf pups and wallaroo joeys. But this was the first time she would spend seventy-two hours straight caring for a baby surrounded by the sights, sounds, and smells of her family. For the next few days, the den would be Harmony's home away from home, until the rest of the team stepped in to help her provide around-the-clock care.

GORILLA DENS

The gorilla dens at the Woodland Park Zoo are in a large indoor area next to the outdoor exhibit. All three of the gorilla family groups at the zoo spend the mornings and evenings there, away from public view. The keepers can close the metal gates and slide see-through doors to divide the space into separate dens. The gorillas use the hay on the floor to make their nests. They also climb up and make nests on high platforms that hang from the walls, the way gorillas in the wild sometimes sleep in the trees.

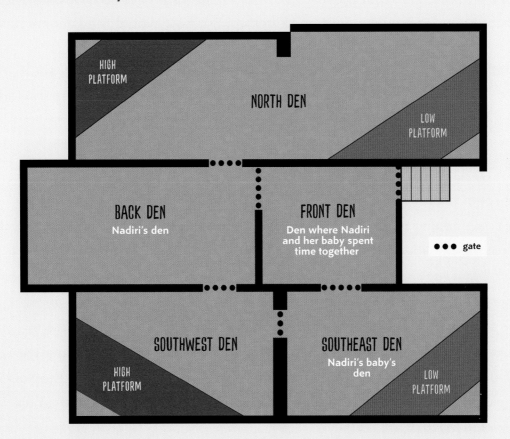

HIGH PLATFORM

NORTH DEN

LOW PLATFORM

BACK DEN

Nadiri's den

FRONT DEN

Den where Nadiri and her baby spent time together

●●● gate

SOUTHWEST DEN

HIGH PLATFORM

SOUTHEAST DEN

Nadiri's baby's den

LOW PLATFORM

The baby began to squirm and make a soft, squawky sound. Harmony gently placed her finger in the baby's mouth, and the baby started to suck on it.

"Let's see if you're hungry enough to take milk from a bottle," said Harmony.

She carried the infant into a small kitchen the keepers had set up next to the den to warm up a bottle of human infant formula. The thirsty infant latched on to the rubber nipple right away and drank the whole bottle. Drowsy from the warm milk, the baby quickly fell asleep in Harmony's arms.

Meanwhile, Judy made a schedule for Nadiri to visit with her baby three times a day: first thing in the morning, before noon, and at the end of the day before the gorillas went to sleep. Judy hoped that these visits would help Nadiri get comfortable enough with her baby that she would want to pick her up. But how would the keepers help her do this?

For safety reasons, the keepers are not allowed inside the den with an adult gorilla. But Judy could still work with Nadiri through a metal gate. Like all the keepers, Judy let

LEARNING TO ACCEPT A BOTTLE

Having spent twenty years of caring for newborn animals at the zoo, Harmony Frazier knew how to feed a baby ape when it was not able to nurse from its mother. "We have found with primate infants, if they are healthy and strong and hungry, they will begin rooting for a nipple. If they have not nursed on their mother, they take to a bottle pretty easily," Harmony explained. "If they have nursed on their mother, then the bottle is a foreign object, and it may take a bit more time to introduce. Out of caution, we will start them with a small amount of Pedialyte—a combination of sweet-tasting water and electrolytes—to test the size of the hole in the nipple and make sure the flow is not too fast. If they manage well, then we will start formula in small amounts."

Nadiri know what she wanted her to do through a combination of words, gestures, pointing a laser light, and food rewards. But Nadiri could choose to cooperate or not.

Judy set up the first visit within hours of the birth. Harmony wrapped the infant in a warm burlap sack and placed her on a bed of hay. Then she left the den. Judy opened the gate between Nadiri and the baby's den.

The tiny gorilla snuggles in the crook of her caregiver's arm.

"Come look at your beautiful baby!" said Judy, pointing near the baby with a small red laser light. Nadiri ventured slowly into the den and took the raisin treat from Judy's hand. Nadiri looked at the baby from a distance and uttered a low-pitched grunt of contentment, or content grunt, a kind of "hello" greeting in gorilla talk. "This is going well," Judy thought.

But when she asked Nadiri to come closer to the baby and touch her, Nadiri refused to budge. Soon the baby began to cry, because she wasn't being held.

"Let's wait a few minutes to see if Nadiri will pick the baby up," Judy whispered to Harmony. But the baby's cries made the new mother anxious, and Nadiri quickly left the den. Judy tried to coax her to come back, but she would not return, so Harmony had to step in to comfort the baby.

The visit had lasted less than five minutes. At least Nadiri trusted the keepers enough to enter the baby's den. But beyond that, she seemed unsure of what to do. Judy had to think of a way to make these visits a good experience for Nadiri and her baby. She hoped that this would give Nadiri the confidence to pick her baby up and nurse her. They had only a few weeks before Nadiri's milk would dry up.

The first few days, Harmony cared for the baby by herself to make sure that she was eating, pooping, and sleeping well. The baby seemed happy as long as she was held. Close physical contact is important for babies to feel safe and secure.

The baby would sleep for three hours at a time and then wake up and demand milk. Harmony let her drink whenever she wanted to. As soon as the baby made a sharp, squawky sound, Harmony prepared a warm bottle of infant formula for her. She weighed the baby every day to make sure she was healthy and growing well. Checking the baby's weight also helped Harmony figure out the right amount of formula to give her.

The gorilla baby can grip tightly with her feet as well as with her hands.

The baby clung to Harmony's furry vest with both hands and feet. Holding on tight would help her build up her strength. But Harmony was ready to grab her if she lost her grip. A protective gorilla mother does something similar: she holds her baby's hand in her mouth when she climbs off the ground, so if the baby lets go, she can keep the baby from falling.

Harmony did her best to imitate a gorilla mother's constant care: grooming her, touching her hands and face, and lifting her by one arm to pick her up so the baby could practice clinging to her back and chest. When it was time for the baby to nap, Harmony would stay with her like a mother shares her nest with her baby. She made a deep purring sound like a gorilla's content grunt to soothe her to sleep.

The first days were difficult, and so were the first nights. Harmony thought the dens would be quieter for the baby when the gorillas were asleep. But both she and the gorillas were in for a surprise.

The gorillas at the zoo were used to a daily routine. All three family groups spent the mornings and evenings in their own areas of the gorilla dens, where they were fed and spent time with their own family group. In the afternoons, each group foraged for food, played, and rested in their outdoor exhibit space, while the dens were cleaned. But they were not used to having a human with them in the dens overnight.

For part of the first few nights, three 400-pound (180 kg) adult male gorillas banged on the doors and made a ruckus with their coughs, hollers, and roars. Harmony felt badly that she was disrupting their sleep. "They must not understand why I am in here and whether they

Nadiri's baby yawns before she goes to sleep. As a newborn, she sleeps three hours at a time and is fed milk whenever she wants it.

An adult male silverback beats his chest and hoots to intimidate an intruder in his territory. He looks scary, but serious fighting among gorillas is rare.

should be concerned," she thought. This change in their nightly routine was probably scary for the gorillas. The silverbacks—the adult male gorillas who were the heads of their families—were just doing their job of protecting the other gorillas in their group.

Gradually, the silverbacks settled down and got used to Harmony being there. Harmony enjoyed the gorilla dens at night, lying in the darkness surrounded by their earthy smell and the sound of the gorillas' deep breathing. She felt proud that they accepted her being there as if she were one of them.

One noontime visit, a few days later, the baby was crying when Nadiri entered the den. To Harmony and Judy's surprise, Nadiri rushed over and softly patted the baby's head. She stayed with the baby for a little while and tucked the burlap blanket around her to quiet her down. Then she went back to the outdoor exhibit space.

GORILLA SMELLS

Gorillas sweat, just as humans do. They also pass gas a lot, due to their high-fiber diet of fruits, leaves, and stems. When a stranger enters a silverback's territory, the silverback will work up a sweat by displaying his strength—beating his chest and strutting—and give off a strong smell. Scientists have recently learned that adult male gorillas can turn up or turn down the strength of their body odor to announce their presence or to signal other gorillas to stay away. The gorilla dens have a strong smell of hay, alfalfa, and sometimes urine and poop. "This might be unpleasant to most people," keeper Judy says, "but for those of us who work with these amazing animals, it smells like home."

"We are seeing some real interest on Nadiri's part," Harmony wrote in the keepers' record book later that day. But would this caring behavior last?

When Harmony's three days of around-the-clock care was up, she chose to continue working the night shift with the baby. From then on, Judy and the rest of the team took turns handling the baby's daytime care.

There was no guidebook for helping a gorilla mother bond with her baby. The keepers had to patiently follow the cues that Nadiri and the baby gave them and build on this mothering behavior when they saw it. But Nadiri's act of soothing the baby was a big breakthrough.

CHAPTER 3
A GROWING BOND

The silverback Leo (*upright*) watches over his family group: Akenji (*left*) and Nadiri (*right*).

Nadiri spent most of her days with the other members of her gorilla family group: Leo, a thirty-seven-year-old silverback, and Akenji, Nadiri's younger half sister. Akenji was much more outgoing and confident than Nadiri. She liked being the center of attention—whether she was playfully wrestling with Leo or sitting next to the outdoor exhibit window, interacting with the public.

Sometimes Akenji seemed to bully Nadiri, forcing her to move if she was sitting where Akenji wanted to be. This dominant display among females is a natural part of gorilla social behavior. Nadiri's acceptance of her sister's actions was a sign of her lower rank in the group. In the wild, the silverback's job as the head of the family is to keep peace in the group. But even the silverback does not intervene between females unless a competition becomes vocal and aggressive. Leo also spent more time with Akenji, and that raised her status in the group even more.

One day in December, Harmony and Judy saw Akenji come up next to Nadiri as she was visiting with her baby through the metal gate. Akenji forced Nadiri to move out of the way so that she could be near the baby. Was Akenji jealous of all the attention the baby was getting, or was she just curious?

After that, the keepers made sure to give Akenji attention in another den while Nadiri was visiting with the baby. The keepers did not consider Akenji's behavior dangerous, just high-spirited. But they wanted Nadiri to have as much time as she could with the baby to trigger her maternal instinct.

Male gorillas become silverbacks around thirteen years of age when the hair on their shoulders and back turns gray or white. Leo is thirty-six years old in this photo.

GORILLA FAMILIES

Gorillas are social animals. They benefit from one another's company in the same ways that human families do. They feel a sense of safety surrounded by their group and learn how to act and communicate by imitating one another.

A gorilla family group is called a troop. In the wild, a troop can include several generations and up to thirty members, but western lowland gorillas tend to live in smaller groups. The silverback is the leader and protector of the family. The troop also includes several adult females and their offspring—juveniles, adolescents, and babies. Young gorillas learn basic skills from their older troop mates—including building a nest, finding food, caring for their siblings, and getting along with one another.

During her night shifts in the gorilla dens, Harmony noticed that the baby had a secret admirer. The silverback Leo calmly watched her from a distance and uttered deep content grunts in her direction while she slept. Leo was not the baby's father. He had been hand-raised at another zoo and spent much of his time with an all-male group before he came to Woodland Park Zoo ten years earlier. Because he had not lived in a family group for very long, he did not have the confident air of a leader that silverbacks normally do.

Harmony began to sit with the baby next to the gate near Leo while he ate to see how the two reacted to each other. When Harmony held the baby up for him to see, Leo shyly looked away. But one day he stuck his finger through the gate that separated them. "Was he trying to make contact with the baby?" Harmony wondered. The wide-eyed baby did not utter a sound. She reacted as calmly to him as Leo had to her. "If the baby could spark a bond with this shy silverback," thought Harmony, "perhaps she could work her magic on Nadiri."

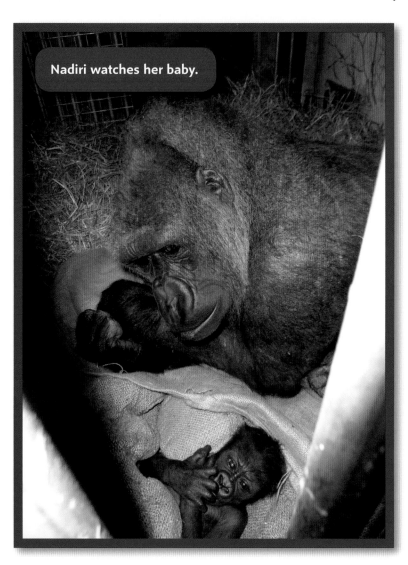

Nadiri watches her baby.

Within a few weeks, Nadiri was acting more curious about her baby. Several times, she came in and lay down nearby just to watch her. Wanting Nadiri to lean in closer, Judy offered her pieces of apple on a spoon right next to the baby's face. Nadiri tried reaching out to take the apple with her hand.

Judy pulled the spoon back. "No, mouth, Nadiri," said Judy, offering the

The baby holds her head up to watch and listen to the sights and sounds around her.

spoon again and urging her to take the apple with her mouth. Nadiri leaned in next to the baby's face and ate the apple. "Good girl," said Judy, pleased that Nadiri understood what Judy needed her to do and had gotten what she wanted.

Gradually and with lots of encouragement, Nadiri grew braver. The time had passed for her to be able to nurse, but Nadiri was calmer now around the baby. The mother started to touch her daughter—exploring her hands, face, and ears. The baby seemed content and alert during Nadiri's visits, propped up in her burlap nest without being held, with sweet-smelling fruits scattered around her.

"I think Nadiri likes the attention she is getting, too," Judy said to Harmony. It was like having a party three times a day with all the special treats and encouragement from the keepers. Judy was determined to spend as much time as she could to help this growing bond between Nadiri and her baby. The more comfortable they became with each other, the sooner Nadiri might pick up her baby.

CHAPTER 4
REACHING OUT

As soon as the baby can sit up, she starts learning to move around and explore her surroundings.

In January, at two months old, the baby was thriving. She weighed eight pounds, had four sharp teeth, and was growing stronger by the day. Harmony and Judy were already seeing the gorilla baby roll back and forth. They helped her sit up and stand up.

During an evening visit with Nadiri, the baby accidentally rolled out of her burlap nest and shrieked in surprise. Judy and Harmony waited to see if Nadiri would pick up her crying baby. But she gently patted the burlap sack the baby was wrapped in and looked nervously at Harmony and Judy as if to say, "Aren't you going to take care of this?"

"Nadiri still seems more comfortable having us handle her baby when she cries," said Harmony, as Nadiri retreated to her den.

"It's a good thing she trusts us," said Judy. "Nadiri needs more time to build up her confidence around the baby so that one day she will decide that picking her up is the best way to soothe her."

COMPARING GORILLA AND HUMAN DEVELOPMENT

Baby gorillas develop almost twice as fast as human babies do in their first year of life. They have to because their gorilla families are constantly on the move—foraging for food and building new nests every day.

Stage	Gorillas	Humans
First teeth	1–2 months	4–6 months
Sitting up	3 months	6–8 months
Walking	4–6 months	9–15 months
Maturity	10–12 years old	18–25 years old

Left: A young western lowland gorilla walks confidently on two feet.
Right: A young boy takes his first steps while his mother watches.

Leo never missed an opportunity to pay attention to the baby. When he saw her clinging to the gate while a keeper was holding her, he calmly approached, put his face right next to the baby's face, and grunted softly at her. The wide-eyed baby did not flinch as Leo gently reached out and touched her tiny fingers with the back of his knuckles.

By three months, the baby could pull herself along the floor by scooting, rolling, and grabbing with her hands. She also began to learn how to climb. Her long, strong arms helped her easily pull herself up.

Every afternoon the baby and her caretakers had the dens to themselves while the adult gorillas were outdoors in the exhibit space. Judy or another keeper watched her carefully to make sure she didn't fall as she tried to climb on a gate or grab onto the jungle gym of canvas hoses hanging from the ceiling. As soon as she lifted herself off the ground, she'd cry out to be rescued. But once she was back in her caretaker's arms, she'd squirm to be let down so she could climb again. Her determined and outgoing personality was starting to show.

Nadiri acted more interested in the baby once she was moving around on her own. The daily visits lasted longer—up to two hours—as Nadiri chose to stay, eat, and rest with her daughter.

The baby liked to watch her mother eat plants with leaves and flowers on them. She would stare at the swaying stems and leaves like a human baby watching a mobile above her crib. As her mother ate the leaves off a forsythia stem, she would scoot in to grab the yellow flowers that fell. It didn't matter that the baby couldn't actually eat solid food yet. Like a young gorilla in the wild, she wanted to imitate whatever her mother was doing.

Sometimes Nadiri would let her have the food to play with. Other times she would utter a soft warning cough to "leave it alone." The baby did as she was told, but she never showed fear toward her mother.

The baby sucks her thumb to calm herself, just like human children do.

One day in late February, the baby was trying to climb the metal gate in her den when Nadiri walked in. The baby reached out her arm to be rescued, as she'd done many times with Harmony and the keepers. But this time, Nadiri scooped the baby off the gate and gently sat down with her in her lap. The baby did not let out a whimper. She clung to her mother's arm for several minutes as they cuddled face-to-face.

Later that day, the keeper proudly wrote in the record book, "FIRST TIME Nadiri pulled Baby into Her Arms & Lap." It had taken almost four months for Nadiri to hold her baby. At last, she was beginning to show mothering behavior.

In March, the zoo held a contest to name the baby gorilla. The name Yola was chosen from fifteen hundred entries. Yola means "firefly" in the Hausa language of West Africa where her great-grandfather Pete had been born. Given the bond she had sparked with Nadiri, Yola's name fit perfectly. But could she count on her mother to protect her when it was time to introduce her to the other members of her family group? And would Yola still be comfortable with Leo once there was no gate separating them?

CHAPTER 5
THE POWER OF TOUCH

Nadiri gives Yola a reassuring pat on the head as Yola practices her walking. Notice the white patch of fur on Yola's rump.

Four-month-old Yola walked on all fours across the den to Judy's open arms. She whimpered as she moved on wobbly legs. But Judy tried not to give in to her complaining and pick her up. The practice was good for Yola.

A small patch of white fur stood out on Yola's rump. This natural marking on a baby gorilla shows up at this age and lasts for several years. It would remind the other gorillas that Yola was still a baby and should be treated with care. In the wild, it also helps mothers keep track of their babies in a group.

None of the other gorillas except Nadiri had been allowed into Yola's den. But at some point, Yola would have to learn how to get along with her family group. Until then, she needed a protector. That is a mother gorilla's job. The keepers had to make sure that the bond between mother and daughter was strong. They also had to make sure that Yola could move through all the dens independently before they would let Leo and Akenji into her space.

Yola spent most of her awake time practicing climbing indoors while Nadiri watched from below. Yola could already pull herself up on the canvas hoses. But as soon as Nadiri moved away, Yola shimmied down and did a fast knuckle-walk over to her mother. She clearly didn't want her mother to be out of her sight.

Nadiri was becoming more attentive to Yola's needs, but Yola demanded her attention too. Yola's soft whimper brought her mother back, and a few content grunts from Nadiri could usually calm Yola down. If not, Nadiri would cover her with a burlap blanket to comfort her and utter a few content grunts as if to say, "You're fine. I'm right here."

Soon Nadiri followed Yola around as the young walker and climber tested her strength while exploring the indoor rooms. Like all gorillas, Yola was amazingly flexible. From wobbly rolls and somersaults to dangling by one arm from the canvas hoses, she was not afraid to take risks with her mother close by.

GORILLA LOCOMOTION

Gorillas mostly knuckle-walk— walk on all fours using their feet and leaning on the knuckles of their hands. Occasionally, gorillas will rear up and walk on their hind feet to see farther or to display when they want to look intimidating. Their long arms and broad chests are strong and flexible like other apes, so they can brachiate—swing from branch to branch in the forest.

Yola practices knuckle-walking on all fours in the outdoor exhibit.

Judy and the other keepers were happy to step back and let Nadiri take charge. But they still helped out at Yola's feeding time. The keepers now asked Nadiri to bring Yola over to the gate several times during the day so they could feed her. Yola had also learned to walk over and take a bottle from them on her own during the night while Nadiri was asleep in a different room.

Late one afternoon in April after a feeding, Judy took Yola outside into the gorilla exhibit space for the first time. The five-month-old held on to Judy's leg as they walked along the dirt paths with tall plants on both sides. They looked up at the trees that towered above. They listened to the whirring sound of an airplane overhead.

Judy felt proud of the animal-care team that had helped Yola grow healthy and strong. She remembered how afraid Nadiri had been around other gorillas when she was five months old. Yola was not afraid of other gorillas because she'd watched them, smelled them, and listened to them communicate with one another in the dens around her from the beginning. Nadiri's steady attentiveness to her daughter was the sign they were waiting for that she was taking charge of her baby. It was time for Yola to walk these dirt paths with her mother so she could learn how to grow up gorilla.

Once Yola is able to move around on her own, she is never far from her mother's side.

Several days later, during Nadiri's afternoon visit, the keepers heard giggling sounds coming from Yola's den. They peeked in just in time to see Nadiri lift Yola by the arm and pull her onto her chest to play. Nadiri made a string of content grunts in a row. It was the first time the keepers had heard the two of them laughing together. After a few minutes, Yola squirmed to get down, and Nadiri let her go.

At five months, Yola had ten teeth and could chew and swallow solid food. One day, as the keepers fed Nadiri a special meal of chopped fruit in front of the baby, Yola's eyes opened wide with excitement. Standing with her face next to Nadiri's, Yola hungrily followed the spoon of fruit until it disappeared into Nadiri's mouth. Between her big spoonfuls, Nadiri let Judy share a few bites of the sweet-smelling fruit with Yola.

At five months, Yola has enough teeth to chew and swallow leafy green vegetables.

Yola's diet was mainly vegetables and fruit. Her favorite foods were crunchy cucumbers, kale, celery, and watermelon. But with her constant teething, Yola put anything and everything in her mouth. The keepers had to take anything that was unsafe out of her mouth, but they were careful of her sharp teeth. Keepers still gave Yola formula in a bottle several times during the day. But now that Yola was eating solid foods, there was no need for them to give her nighttime feedings.

Nadiri relaxes with Yola, lying in the soft straw of her den floor.

Judy was eager to try having Nadiri and Yola spend the night together in the same den. That evening, Judy and another keeper placed Yola in Nadiri's den and ducked out of Yola's sight. At first, the keepers heard Yola cry and fuss while Nadiri gathered hay for a nest. Nadiri then tried holding her and covering her with her burlap blanket. But Yola would not calm down.

"Yola's probably confused by the new situation," Judy whispered to the other keeper. "Wondering when we are coming to take her back to her den." Nadiri remained patient and attentive to Yola the whole time she cried. Finally, the exhausted baby fell asleep.

The next morning, the keepers found the two gorillas calmly resting in Nadiri's nest. From then on, Yola and Nadiri stayed together at night. The only time the two were apart was for a few hours in the afternoon when Nadiri joined Leo and Akenji outdoors in the exhibit space.

Yola turned six months old in May. The bond between mother and daughter was strong. It was time for Yola to meet the rest of her family. The keepers decided to introduce Leo first. Leo had always acted calmly around Yola, while Akenji had shown jealousy toward the baby. But this would be a test for Nadiri. While she was gentle and attentive to her baby, she had never picked Yola up and carried her as a protective gorilla mother would. "Would that protective instinct kick in," wondered Judy, "with a 400-pound [180 kg] silverback and her daughter in the same room?"

Yola learns by watching her mother closely.

Early the next morning, the keepers opened the sliding doors in the gorilla dens to create a larger space for Leo's visit. They invited Leo into the back half of a shared room separated by fencing from where Yola and Nadiri usually stayed. To the keepers' amazement, as soon as Nadiri saw Leo enter the room, she picked Yola up and carried her against her chest to a different room out of Leo's sight. Clearly, she was uncomfortable with Leo being so near them and felt responsible for keeping her baby safe. Everyone's eyes filled with tears. This was exactly what they had hoped for.

The second day, the keepers removed the fencing. Leo seemed nervous when he entered the space. The shy silverback made a short display announcing his presence as he walked past Yola and Nadiri. Then he climbed up to his favorite platform bed and voiced content grunts at them from a distance for the rest of the visit. Now that there was no barrier between them, Yola seemed curious to meet Leo. But Nadiri wasn't ready to allow her to approach him. Before Yola could take a step, Nadiri picked her up and carried her out of the room.

Leo is the silverback leader of his family group.

Nadiri scoops Yola into her arms.

Over the next week, Leo, Yola, and Nadiri gradually grew more comfortable with one another. Leo would amble by them to pick up a leafy bamboo branch to eat and sit down near them without Nadiri moving away. The keepers were not surprised that Leo acted calm and respectful. And they were thrilled to see Nadiri being protective of Yola like a mother gorilla should. But would her protective behavior last when her feisty sister Akenji walked into the room?

CHAPTER 6
A FAMILY AT LAST

Leo (*front*) forages for food, with Yola and Nadiri close behind him.

On a beautiful morning in May, Yola woke up to find both Nadiri and Leo sitting peacefully with her in the den. Nadiri sat next to her. But Yola's focus was on Leo. Judy was giving him a daily hand treatment for an old injury through the bars. As soon as the treatment ended, the keepers opened the moving doors and let Akenji into the den.

The two sisters exchanged content grunts as Akenji joined the group. But Akenji wasted no time seeking out the main attraction. She marched right up to Yola and grabbed the burlap blanket she was sitting on. Nadiri quickly moved away from her sister. While Akenji sniffed and inspected the blanket, Yola followed her mother. But as the baby gorilla walked by her aunt, Akenji reached out and gave her a little push on the rump.

Yola shrieked and raced to her mother's side. Akenji looked confused. Was she just being curious, the keepers wondered, or was she testing the new baby to see how she would react?

Either way, Akenji seemed determined to make contact with Yola. Several times she stepped up and beat her chest in a display of strength that made Yola shriek louder. That got Leo's attention! Leo stood up, gave an angry bark and threat grunt, and ran toward Akenji, forcing her to move away.

Akenji surveys the outdoor exhibit area by standing upright on a swinging vine and reaching for a nearby branch to balance herself.

GORILLA TALK

Gorillas use many different sounds and gestures to communicate with one another. Each sound and gesture has its own special meaning. For example, a silverback might belch or hum when he is enjoying a patch of tasty berries. A hoot could be a signal to others in the troop that danger is near. While gorillas baring their teeth might look threatening, it is actually a sign of submissiveness. But open-mouth grins showing no teeth (or just the upper teeth) are meant to be playful and show their playmates that they won't bite.

This sharp rebuke from the silverback was a warning to Akenji that she needed to calm down. Silverbacks in the wild actively protect their young. Even though Leo was not Yola's father, he showed the group that he would help Nadiri look out for Yola if Akenji behaved too aggressively.

The keepers were delighted to see Leo take on the silverback role as a protector and peacekeeper in the family. They believed his fatherly attentiveness to Yola and willingness to step in when Akenji got too rambunctious would make things easier for Nadiri when the family group was finally together in the outdoor exhibit space.

Nadiri and Yola sat close to Leo for the rest of Akenji's visit. Mostly, Akenji acted more restrained, though she did get a few pokes in. Yola cried out, but this time Leo and Nadiri

When the family is together outside in the exhibit space, Nadiri and Yola often sit near Leo (*left*) for protection from the rambunctious Akenji.

Adventurous and always curious, Yola flexes her muscles in play as she hangs upside down from a fallen branch.

did not react. Akenji had been clearly warned. Perhaps they considered these last jabs just a good-natured tease among family members.

In June, Yola turned seven months old and weighed nearly 20 pounds (9 kg). She drank formula from a cup, because she was too impatient to suck from a bottle. Nadiri and Yola spent most of the day outside in the warm summer weather. Yola followed Nadiri down the dirt paths, browsing on leaf buds and green branches that were just coming out. Confident and much more independent now, Yola was ready to taste everything this outdoor world had to offer.

Sometimes, Akenji followed Nadiri and Yola around and beat her chest as she passed them. When Akenji sat down near Yola, Nadiri would immediately pick up her baby and move away. Leo sat on the hill above them, quietly watching over the group. Both he and Nadiri were always on the alert when Akenji was on the move.

Nadiri watches Yola feast on her favorite buttercups and enjoy the spring blooms.

Nadiri often sat near Leo so he could intervene if Akenji made a sudden move toward Yola. The keepers were thrilled to see this new connection between them. Leo was acting like a silverback would in the wild, and Nadiri seemed more relaxed and confident around him. Mothering Yola had clearly raised Nadiri's rank in the group.

For now, Yola seemed happy playing in her patch of clover, chasing butterflies, and eating the shiny petals off buttercups. Under the watchful eye of her mother and surrounded by her family, Yola was safe and loved.

WE ARE FAMILY!

- Gorillas and humans share 97.7 percent of the same genes. They belong to the same primate group, called hominids. Like humans, gorillas have large skulls and big brains to store information, thirty-two teeth, flexible fingers and toes, and opposable thumbs. They also have opposable toes to grasp food and to help them climb. Gorillas can grow as tall as humans are, but they weigh three times as much.

- Gorillas and humans have different bone structures, and these differences affect the way they live. Gorilla pelvises tip forward, which makes it easy to knuckle-walk on all fours, but standing up straight is difficult. Human pelvises are shaped like a basket, which makes it easier for humans to stand up straight. Human legs are longer than gorillas, so humans can run farther. But gorilla arms are longer, so they're able to reach high for fruit and swing from the trees.

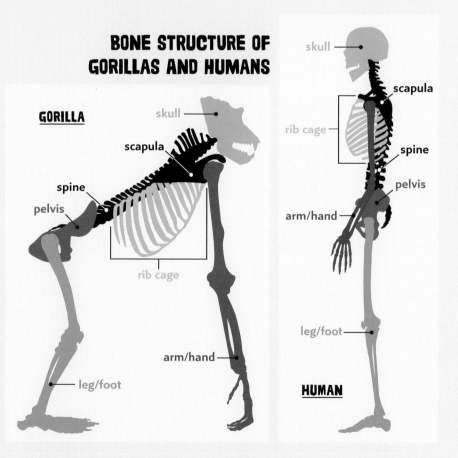

BONE STRUCTURE OF GORILLAS AND HUMANS

GORILLA

skull
scapula
spine
pelvis
rib cage
arm/hand
leg/foot

skull
scapula
rib cage
spine
pelvis
arm/hand
leg/foot

HUMAN

PROTECTING GORILLAS AROUND THE WORLD

- The four gorilla subspecies are the western lowland gorilla (*Gorilla gorilla gorilla*), the Cross River gorilla (*Gorilla gorilla diehli*), the eastern lowland gorilla (*Gorilla beringei graueri*), and the mountain gorilla (*Gorilla beringei beringei*). In the wild, gorillas are critically endangered—at extreme risk of dying out. The western lowland gorilla once had the largest population. It has declined over 60 percent in the last twenty years to about ninety-five thousand. Large swaths of their habitat have been lost because of logging, mining, and large-scale farming by humans. Gorillas are hunted illegally for food and injured by traps set for other animals. They can also catch human diseases, such as the Ebola virus, which has killed many gorillas.

- Few studies have been done of gorillas in the wild because they live in remote areas. It's difficult to find and follow gorilla groups in the dense forests. Biologist George B. Schaller made the first in-depth study of the mountain gorilla in 1959. Ten years later, primatologist Dian Fossey lived among mountain gorillas to study them. She wrote a book about them called *Gorillas in the Mist*. These early conservation efforts helped people understand the important roles gorillas play in the balance of nature and the serious threats to their survival.

- Since 1995, the Mbeli Bai Study of more than 440 western lowland gorillas living in Nouabale-Ndoki National Park in the Republic of the Congo has helped researchers learn more about gorilla behavior. They've discovered new facts, such as their use of tools to get food. They also keep track of the number of gorillas living in the *bai* (the clearing). They're encouraged because eleven gorilla babies were born there in 2018 alone. Zoos like Woodland Park Zoo support this ongoing study as part of their conservation mission to promote the long-term survival of all gorillas in zoos and around the world.

- African sanctuaries such as the Fernan-Vaz Gorilla Project and the Projet Protection des Gorilles in Gabon rescue and treat gorillas orphaned by poachers. Besides protecting the gorillas in their care, these sanctuaries help to socialize young gorillas with the older gorillas. Eventually, they will be reintroduced to the wild in groups. The goal, according to the World Conservation Union, is to establish a self-sustaining population of western gorillas in the wild.

- You can help gorillas by donating your used cellphones or other handheld electronics to zoos. The ore needed to make these devices energy-efficient is mined in the Congo, home to gorillas. To save the gorillas' habitat from being destroyed by mining, many zoos have programs that recycle handheld electronics. Visit https://www.eco-cell.com for more information.

GORILLA HABITATS
- Western lowland gorilla
- Cross River gorilla
- Eastern lowland gorilla
- Mountain gorilla

AUTHOR'S NOTE

Helping a mother gorilla successfully bond with her baby after she refused to care for her at birth is a rare accomplishment in the zoo world. It was amazing to meet and interview the gorilla keepers and infant-care staff who worked so patiently for many months to bring Nadiri and her daughter, Yola, together. But what surprised and delighted us all was seeing the shy silverback Leo play such an important role in Yola's young life.

Unfortunately, Leo died in 2018. At forty years old, he had already lived ten years longer than most male gorillas in the wild. Yola was only two and a half when she lost her surrogate father, but Leo's gentle and protective behavior showed her what it means to be part of a gorilla family. Because she was raised around gorillas from birth, Yola's bond with Leo and Nadiri will guide her as she grows up and one day has a baby of her own. We miss you, Leo, but your memory lives on in the pages of this book.

Leonel, or Leo as he was fondly called, 1978–2018

ACKNOWLEDGMENTS AND SOURCES

Thank you to the staff at Woodland Park Zoo who so graciously shared their time and expertise with me. I conducted interviews with them between June 2016 and March 2018, and all direct quotations in this book came from these interviews.

This book would not have been possible without you: Judy Sievert, gorilla keeper and patient teacher in response to my many questions; Harmony Frazier, senior veterinary technician and tireless advocate for all animal species; Dr. Darin Collins, director of animal health, and mammal curator Martin Ramirez, for giving me such an excellent overview early on; Gigi Allianic, public relations manager, for arranging the interviews; and Rebecca Whitham, associate director of communications, and Jeremy Dwyer-Lindgren, photographer and video coordinator, for their cooperation in providing photographs for the book.

I would also like to thank gorilla keeper Stephanie Paine-Jacobs for her insightful blog article, "Becoming a Silverback: Leo's Story," and gorilla keepers Rachel Vass and Traci Colwell and director of animal care Nancy Hawkes for their comments and corrections on the manuscript.

Special thanks to Patty Peters at Columbus Zoo for arranging my February 2016 interview with the amazing animal care team and Surrogacy Program coordinators Barbara Jones and Maureen Casale, for their willingness to share their strategies for successful baby gorilla care.

Thanks also to my fearless agent, Anne Depue, the enthusiastic support of editorial director Carol Hinz at Millbrook Press, and her wonderful editor Susan Rose. And finally, a grateful shout-out to photographer and Yola fan Judy Ryan for being there week after week at the gorilla exhibit taking fantastic photos of her favorite gorilla family.

—Clare Hodgson Meeker

GLOSSARY

adolescent: a young animal developing into an adult

airway: the passage between the mouth and the lungs, which needs to be open to breathe

bond: to form a close relationship with someone, especially a parent with a baby

browse: the tender shoots, twigs, leaves, and fruit of shrubs—and eating those shoots, twigs, leaves, and fruit

conservation: the protection of animals, plants, and natural resources

content grunt: a kind of "hello" greeting or soothing sound in gorilla talk

contractions: muscles working in preparation for birth

display: a gorilla showing strength by beating the chest and strutting

endangered: a species at risk of dying out

exhibit space: an area in a zoo where people can see animals

family group: a group of gorillas that interacts like a family, which can include a silverback, other adults, juveniles, adolescents, and infants

formula: a milk mixture for feeding an infant that is similar to mother's milk

grooming: to clean another animal or oneself

habitat: the natural home of a plant or animal

hand-raised: a zoo animal raised by humans rather than by animals of its own species

instinct: a natural ability to do something that doesn't have to be learned. Some animals are born with all the instincts they need to survive. Others need to learn survival skills.

juvenile: a young animal that is not yet fully grown

knuckle-walk: to walk on all fours using feet and leaning on the knuckles of hands

labor: giving birth

maternal instinct: a natural ability to protect and raise young

nurse: a baby or young animal drinking milk from the mother's body

poaching: hunting or killing animals illegally

primate: an animal species that have fur or hair, can use their hands, and make milk for their young, which includes humans, apes, and monkeys

silverback: an adult male gorilla who is the head of his family group

species: one kind of living thing

subspecies: a group of related plants or animals that is smaller than a species

surrogate: a substitute parent who protects and raises young as a parent would

One-year-old Yola deftly uses her hands and feet to climb up a vine in the outdoor exhibit.

MORE ABOUT GORILLAS

Books

Applegate, Katherine. *Ivan: The Remarkable True Story of the Shopping Mall Gorilla*. New York: Clarion, 2014. This illustrated picture book presents the true story of a gorilla who was captured in the wild as a baby and spent twenty-seven years alone in a cage at a shopping mall in Washington State. Thanks to a large public protest and help from Woodland Park Zoo, Ivan was moved to the Atlanta Zoo and spent the rest of his life with other gorillas.

Marsic, Katie. *The Most Endangered Gorillas*. New York: Scholastic, 2017. Read more about gorillas in the wild and their importance in the natural world.

Nippert-Eng, Christine. *Gorillas Up Close*. New York: Henry Holt, 2016. This photo-filled book profiles a gorilla family troop and describes the habitat design and gorilla training at Chicago's Lincoln Park Zoo.

Turner, Pamela. *Gorilla Doctors: Saving Endangered Great Apes*. Boston: Houghton Mifflin Harcourt, 2008. Follow along as a group of scientists provides emergency care to mountain gorillas in Rwanda and Uganda and foster parent an orphaned gorilla.

Websites

Aspinall Foundation's Project in Gabon
https://www.berggorilla.org/en/home/news-archive/article-view/the-aspinall-foundations-project-in-gabon/
Learn about a unique western lowland gorilla rehabilitation and reintroduction project in the forests of southeastern Gabon by Projet Protection des Gorilles.

Fernan-Vaz Gorilla Project
http://gorillasgabon.org/
This sanctuary in Gabon, Africa, works to rescue and reintroduce orphaned gorillas to the wild, provides jobs for local people, and raises awareness of the importance of gorillas in the environment.

Mbeli Bai Study

https://www.mbelibaistudy.org

Find out more about this ongoing study of gorillas in the wild and about Club Ebobo, connecting youth with conservation. (*Ebobo* means "gorilla" in the local language.)

Pan African Sanctuary Alliance (PASA)

https://pasaprimates.org/about-gorillas/

This nonprofit organization, based in Portland, Oregon, helps twenty-three sanctuaries in Africa share resources and educate the public about their work in the fight to save wild gorillas, chimpanzees, and orangutans from extinction.

Woodland Park Zoo Blog: "Grow with Yola"

http://blog.zoo.org/2017/11/grow-with-yola-hello-two.html

Visit this site for the latest news, photos, and videos of Yola.

Videos

The Woodland Park Zoo created these video to share updates about baby Yola's growth and development during her first months of life:

"And Our Baby Gorilla's New Name Is . . ."
https://www.youtube.com/watch?v=5AMqxJ5zTcE

"Baby Gorilla Continues to Thrive"
https://www.youtube.com/watch?v=4ey6c32QVww

"Baby Gorilla Gets a Veterinary Check Up"
https://www.youtube.com/watch?v=WRYM3qQ_Gjg

"Gorilla Baby Yola Bonds with Mother Nadiri"
https://www.youtube.com/watch?v=6GOujS6wC7Y

"Grow with Yola: Woodland Park Zoo Baby Gorilla"
https://www.youtube.com/watch?v=24paMMf1VWE

INDEX

PHOTO ACKNOWLEDGMENTS

Special thanks to the Woodland Park Zoo for providing photos for this book.

Additional images: Robert Sorbo, p. 5; Clare Hodgson Meeker, p. 6 (top left); Judy Ryan, pp. 31, 36, 45; Douglas Magno/AFP/Getty Images, p. 8; Laura Westlund/Independent Picture Service, pp. 11, 39, 41; hypergurl/Getty Images, p. 16; Jurgen & Christine Sohns/FLPA/Science Source, p. 23 (left); skynesher/Getty Images, p. 23 (right); Milan M/Shutterstock.com (design texture).

Cover: Jeremy Dwyer-Lindgren/Woodland Park Zoo.